GOD, THE DEVIL, AND THE SNEAKY ENGINEER: QUOTATIONS FROM NATHAN COPPEDGE

BY NATHAN COPPEDGE

INTRODUCTORY NOTE

NATHAN COPPEDGE HAS ALSO SPOKEN OR WRITTEN UNDER A VARIETY OF DIFFERENT PERSONALITIES, SUCH AS IN PREVIOUS LIVES, AND BY FAKING OTHER PEOPLE'S QUOTES. THROUGH THIS METHOD HIS INFLUENCE HAS BECOME FAR MORE POWERFUL THAN YOU MIGHT EXPECT FOR SOMEONE OF HIS DEMEANOR OR CLASS.

THE FOLLOWING SECTIONS OF QUOTES COME NOT ONLY FROM NATHAN COPPEDGE'S PRIMARY WRITINGS, BUT ALSO FROM COPPEDGE'S PREVIOUS LIVES AND ALTER-EGOES.

IN SOME CASES I FIND IT APPROPRIATE TO ELABORATE THE LIVES OF THESE CHARACTERS, AS FROM WHAT I KNOW FEW HAVE READ ABOUT THEM IN THEIR GENUINE FORM, AND THUS, THESE NOTES HAVE ANECDOTAL VALUE CONCERNING KEY ELEMENTS IN HISTORY.

FOR EXAMPLE, DID YOU KNOW THAT AARON BURR AND MARIE D' ANTOINETTE WERE BOTH SPIES FOR THE BRITISH? OR THAT THE CHIEF EGYPTIAN

GOD BELIEVED IN 'ONE ALMIGHTY GOD' BECAUSE HE HAD DIRECT EVIDENCE? OR THAT THE WORD 'GILGAMESH' WAS INVENTED BY A YOUNG 'SORCERER' TO AVOID GETTING ABUSED BY STRONG MEN, THE SAME YOUNG SORCERER WHO INVENTED THE REFRAIN 'WEE WEE WEE, ALL THE WAY HOME', EXCEPT IN ANCIENT SUMERIAN?

THESE FACTS MAY NOT BE BELIEVABLE TO ALL, BUT CONSIDERING NATHAN'S INTELLIGENCE AND ABILITY WITH APHORISMS, IT IS A CLOSE CALL. NOTABLY, HIS CURRENT LIFE IS HIS LEAST SEDITIOUS AND MOST INTELLECTUAL, A FACT THAT MAY BE STRANGELY TELLING ABOUT THE WAYS HE HAS WEEDLED HIS WAY OUT OF HIS FATE IN THE PAST, INCLUDING ONE TIME HE LIVED AT LEAST 400 YEARS---AS A CHINESE GOD!

HERE IS THE STORY OF THE MISCHIEF I WREAKED THROUGHOUT HISTORY---ALSO THE STORY OF A REFORMED INTELLECTUAL.

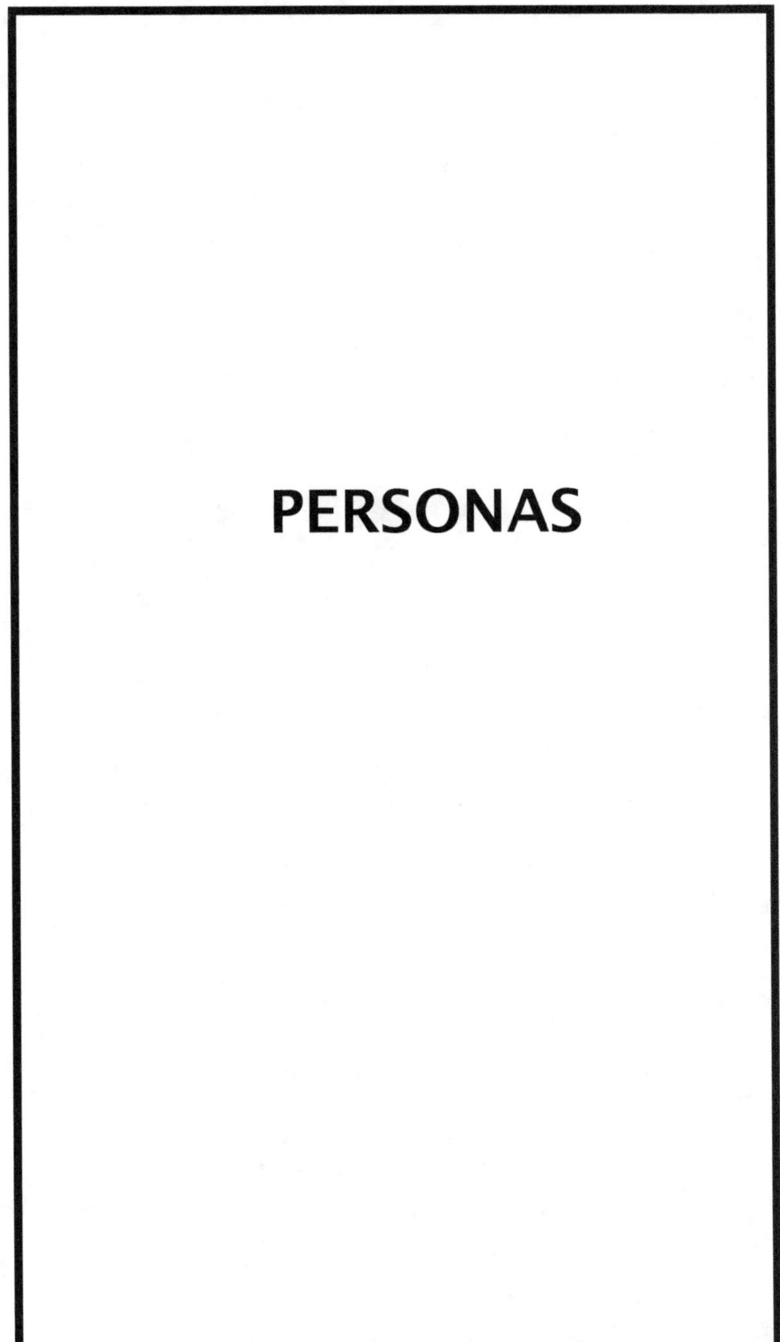

PERSONAS

AARON BURR

THE LIFE OF AARON BURR INCLUDING KEY QUOTATIONS

There was a young man named Todd Oxbridge, well it turned out that I was him;

My family made a point that I was too foolish to go to Cambridge, and I believed them; Others of them had been there, great scholars; Going to Cambridge was no mean achievement; But I took it literally;

I was interviewed at Oxford and spouted language uncontentiously; It was a time when anyone from a noble family, as I was, could make by at being uncontentious;

'Console deux' said someone;

'I thought it meant amour d' esperit' I said;

'While you're in England, you should really consider visiting Bedlam';

'Oh?';

'You're French aren't you? I could hear your accent';

'My name is Todd, actually. Todd Oxbridge. I'm from a noble family. I will consider that';

He muttered under his breath ‘Well, not if you’re noble’ I pretended not to hear him;

I went anyway; I traveled the next day; I went in ticketed carriage, being advised not to hire my own; Too many ruffians; Upon setting foot, I was robbed, but not robbed blind; I had stuffed money in every shoe and crevice; And rumor had it that ruffians sometimes left their visitors senseless; I was lucky;

I returned to Oxford, where I could overhear someone saying: ‘That’s Todd Oxbridge. Such a fool and so outspoken’

When I related my experience he said ’There, we thought you were a fool, but you weren’t robbed blind’ The story was oft-repeated; I decided to shut my mouth and devote myself to study;

A man at Oxford offered Todd Oxbridge an interview. They toured the Tower of London, which was then still operating.

“You may like this idea. You may detest this idea. I’m offering you a job --- as a spy” said the mysterious man.

“Do you accept? I know you‘re a bit of a dandy” he said. “But it should be light work. As a condition of acceptance, you are to take a new name----a nom d‘ etre so to speak. And you should know French…”

“My name is Aaron Burr, and I accept!”

"How about the French?" the man said.

"Pereille l' plur" Burr stuttered.

"Perfect" the man said.

Now the mysterious man continued. His voice dropped to a conspiratorial tone, if it had not already. Burr could barely hear him.

"As a spy, you will be in no mean spit of trouble. You should practice warfare, like this---!"

And he stabbed a sword into the wall of the tower, yielding a loud, strangled scream.

(The oublettes held prisoners who were mortared into the wall, held there until they were starved or killed by their captors).

Aaron Burr left as soon as he had information about travel arrangements. He was in a tight spot for money. He thought his French would manage.

The ship left almost immediately, and Burr felt blessed with health on the voyage. He felt hardly ill at all, for almost three weeks into the traveling. Then the rotten food began to nag at him. But, they arrived. He would have no escort by the Navy on this voyage. It was top secret.

He was instructed by his coordinator to get a sense of the "local varieties" --- the people who dwelled here. Not long after, he found himself lost in the wilderness of Virginia.

"Par l' Vouz Francais?" he said.

It was an American military commander.

Burr offered his assistance as a French speaker who "might be of useful service to the commander."

Soon he was in close quarters with the Americans, who said he wasn't allowed to have a pistol (he felt in need of self-defense, and remembered what the mysterious man had said about combat. Surely he wasn't supposed to take all of these men on by himself?). Then he remembered something about 'informo-lecturalese' and managed to grab a few papers from the Americans before he set out for his assigned work for the them.

However, he didn't get far before the Americans caught him, and labeled him a double-agent. He spent time in prison, while a decision was reached between parties about what to do---honorably speaking.

Since he was a spy, and a spy was the biggest disgrace, he was taken back to an island held by the British. The British had agreed to execute him by firing squad. It was the grittiest experience of his life. He could see the sweat on the uniforms, and the muskets lining up and being rammed with powder. There was an intense pain, and a blinding light, but it was immediately over. Some sharpshooter had been clever enough to get him through the eye socket. There it was---the surprisingly graceful end of a life that was supposed to be clever, the life of Aaron Burr, otherwise known as the fool named Todd Oxbridge.

QUOTES BY AARON BURR

"That's fine stuff. That's fine stuff no matter wot, I realized."

Aaron Burr also wrote about trickery in the following way:

(1) If something looks bad, try your luck. A better place may look less comfortable.

(2) If you succeed, do not dwell on success. Change your footing, and do not transgress.

(3) Travel to a place where people believe your story.

(4) If you fail, announce that you are a fool. Then quickly mingle.

(5) Words are an aid in the quest for knowledge. The simplest words make others talk about complicated matters. Complex words do the reverse.

(6) Make sounds appropriate to nobody, and no one will think you're any harm at all. This works with tact as well.

(7) Trade names as necessary, but only when you need to get on even footing.

(8) Work out a map of the land, and keep it secret. No one will believe you have a secret.

(9) Attempt to work out the nature of characters you pass by. Other people will think you're working on a novel.

(10) You will become popular, if you're not too much of a dandy.

(11) If you are hungry, trick people into giving you food for others. There are always beggars who are more deserving. The belly must be fed.

(12) Looks are virtuous. Shed all clothing that looks like rags, and steal as necessary from the banks of the rivers. If no fine clothing is found, a beggar's will do.

(13) Otherwise, do not make victims of others. Trespassing against others' will induces risk.

(14) Create a fabric or false veil of evil to test others' commitments. (If you know what is going on, then you have the ability to control others).

(15) This was crossed out, but concerned working for both sides of the war.

ANN BOLYN

The first or second life that I remember as a woman. Also the first or second life in which I remember being beheaded.

Essentially, the king said I was a 'too clever woman from France'.

I said: "I'm too clever for you, and I'm not a little cleverer I'm proud to say".

He got angry that I had talked about a cleaver, and got to talking how I had rolled in a cart of hay with someone from the village.

I said: "I haven't got one gray hair, have I, from the peasants in the village, and I don't nay like a horse like I'm fit for a horse".

The scene became more ridiculous, until he thought I had eyes for the cupbearer.

"The cup bearer, don't be ridiculous, he's not even a man!"

And he said: "Well, now I know you've been fishing in the village".

And he gave someone an evil wink.

Then he asked me how I would like to be executed.

And I said, I'd like my head cut clean off like a good woman.

And he said, that would be his pleasure. Or really the executioner's pleasure when it came down to it. He didn't see any pleasure in it.

And I said: "Well, if you don't see any pleasure in it, why have your way with it?"

And he said "You're a whore."

And I said: "In France when we say whore, we mean that we're from Hell"

And he said: "There you have it!"

Then he had me marshaled off to prison.

ASTON-I-SHED

In a past life Nathan Coppedge believe he was an Egyptian God who was given a puzzle by "the real God" to create a problem for Mankind. Aston-i-shed's solution was to create matter in outer space. It felt foolish, but for this he was remembered as the chief, creator god of Egypt. These are his quotations, remembered in English.

"Watch and I will tell you: the success of the entertainer is being entertained. The consciousness of the perceiver is the Eye of Ra. The fortune of the muses is made of gold. The monster of the oceans is made of sand. The chimera holds fortunes yet untold"---Aston-I-Shed

"Before nature, before law I burned like a bird of fire."---Aston-I-Shed

"The evening is when everything began."---Aston-I-Shed

"The sun sank into the sea, and gave birth to eternity."---Aston-I-Shed

"The sun is a firey bird."---Aston-I-Shed

"Everything new is better at being old."---Aston-I-Shed

"Truths that are young are better at being told."---Aston-I-Shed

"Death is transcient. It is white like the sun."---Aston-I-Shed

"Someday the dirt of the earth will burn away."---Aston-I-Shed

"Of course I'm much more learned than my knowledge."---Aston-I-Shed

CHILDHOOD

These first quotes come from my childhood. I was a very quiet child. But, my thoughts were profound in their range of significance. Time and ultimate belief are important concepts for me during this period.

"Estoy Muerto / I'm dead
so I'm death"

"I don't believe in God,
And I don't believe in
the Devil either"

GODDESS POSTERITY

This was a figure virtually invented by Nathan Coppedge to fill in missing historical quotations. It is a standard of perfection, and also tends to be Neo-Classical in character. A rule is not to refer to any of the people, events, or beliefs of Nathan Coppedge, but instead state objective facts regarding matters of vast historical importance, even to the point of mystery or inscrutability.

“Things like language proliferate, and with them, a wide variety of logics----or other, far more obscure terms.” ---Posterity

"There’s no typical answer about opinions on silence!" ---Posterity\

“Wise age is the succor of evil---said Posterity in an evil mood”

"Some novelty is a pragmatic answer" ---Posterity

“Where is a reality a contradiction? Where systems have not emerged” ---Posterity

"Fate is an interrupted dream /
That knows not where to cast her eye…"
---Posterity

"Treating a field of some substance ambiguously can be a way to evoke the elemental difference"

GOD-IN-THE-BOX

“Its a human game, this god-in-the-box
but you ask any one and he says that he's lost.
Who says rhyming can‘t be a name-game?
What if it‘s the game of God?
Who would know, if God played with himself?
He could play some dialectic---
Make people wiser,
Replace sex with wisdom,
Paint the sky brighter!
That could be God----
Like a God-in-the-Box!
Maybe surprise you,
Because I think he is lost!
But everything comes down to that:
God-in-the-Box!”

God Peeing Poem

“We must think it’s fast to think it’s slow…

Or ever after always go…”

INVENTOR OF THE WORD 'GILGAMESH'

It was in Ancient Sumer, and there were not many buildings. Competitions took place for receiving the few benefits that were available, such as grain and clean clothing. In the midst of this rather simple, yet oppressive climate, a young man made a kind of name for himself amongst the illiterate people of the time, by conning the strong men into thinking he could turn them into pigs, etc. It was a short-lived fame, as soon the strong-men took the name Gilgamesh, which he had invented to intimidate them, as a name for their hero, forever perpetuating the value of the strong-man body-type.

"He is Gilgamesh and he is Gilgamesh. I'm a sorcerer. Now I'm going to disappear"---The Inventor of the Word 'Gilgamesh'

"I don't know any good tricks. You should see me play dirty. I don't"---The Inventor of the Word 'Gilgamesh'

"You die, I die. I'm thrice dead. You

die, I die laughing. You cry 'wee wee wee wee, all the way home"---The Inventor of the Word 'Gilgamesh'

"I didn't turn him into a cow, I turned him into a pig. And he cried like a pig (I invented 'the joke' about his generalities)"---The Inventor of the Word 'Gilgamesh'

KWANG GUO

He gave a look, as if to say: these flowers are enchanted.
>“I can make them wither” he said.
<“I don’t see them withering” someone
said.
>“What about this one” he said
And it immediately turned black.
“You didn’t touch it” someone said.
“I didn’t need to touch it, because I
had the power” he said.

>“I defeat all by having all compete.
My champion
Is the winner because I am the cham-
pion of kung-fu.

I do not fight. See: you have your
weaknesses.
You fight, you die. I do not say that I
am god”

<“But you say you are Kung Wu” said
the fighter.

>“I do not say I am Kung Wu, because I
am Kung Wu”

<“Then, let’s fight”

>“Yes, let’s fight. When I say let’s
fight, then you fight
other men. That’s how I fight”

<“That’s a chicken-legged god”

>“I have died before. Now you fight,
you win”

<“I don’t want to fight. I want to be
god”

>“You don’t want to fight. You still get
a prize” (evil wink)
Aside: “give him a lot of money. Then
have him killed”

Other man: “Killed. No, master Wu. Not
killed”

>“I have been killed before. This is
how he becomes god”

At a different time:

“Don’t ever kill me. I do not die. That
is how
I am Kung Wu”

“There is such a thing as try,
There is such a thing as die----
There I do not go!”

"Dogs do not eat!
I am a dog!
I am not a man!
So I am god
God I do not say
I tricked you!
I did not say what I said!
The words are the opposite of what they mean!
It is the opposite things which happen!
The opposite meanings say almost anything!"

"There are two people.
One knows what he knows, and it is him
One does not know Master Kuo, and it is not him.
How can one know and not know?
How can one by him and not him?
If I know him, I am him!
If I do not know him, I am not him!"
At that moment, he disappeared.

"If they define me or not-him, they might succeed.
But it does not serve me like it does

other people"

He may have been one of the first to say:

"If I hadn't already"

And,

"I have not eaten for days"

"Just because it's a story
doesn't mean it isn't true---!"

"I'm not saying they're not more intelligent (gods).
Perhaps time has passed (for me)!
Would they argue?"

"Some say Chinese literature was lost---
You say it was not---!
All I have is the mandate of heaven in English!"

"Invisible is invincible.
I wouldn't want them to suffer."
(Said of dragons and emperors.
An incredible joke since they
wouldn't have suffered otherwise).
---Kwang Guo

MARIE D' ANTOINETTE

By this time in history, Nathan Coppedge was an Egyptian god, so he was though of as a devil. Nonetheless, he was forced from body to body. Sometimes he was a woman, like Ann Bolyn or, in this case Marie Antoinette. However, Marie Antoinette was more self-absorbed than cruel. If she had it her way, anyone could live the life she lived. That was her basic moral. If people didn't agree with her, they must want to suffer. So, she was remembered as a devil in a time when suffering seemed unavoidable. What she thought of this is that, relative to the poor she knew how to have fun. But she wasn't a god. Not anymore. That was her attitude when greeting other nobility. With the poor, she played games, like stealing their hair, or entertaining them with the violin. She thought violins meant violence, and that stealing hair was the kind of game the poor would appreciate. After all, they didn't seem to know that suffering was bad----they didn't know it enough to be god, anyway. (But in later lives, Nathan learned to be poor, relative to the life of Marie Antoinette. To compensate, the gods allowed him to have significant cleanliness, which, he realized, hardly anyone was ever aware of before that. Consequently, Nathan became democratic. And then, he became schizophrenic. But this is the story of Marie d' Antoinette, Queen of France, and virtual inventor of palindromes, which she named after an early-life experience she called prostitution. She was a very modern woman for her time, and perhaps even a careless spy for England. She was tricked into believing that all nobles are spies, something that is carefully left out of the story).

THE LIFE OF MARIE D' ANTOINETTE, AS COPPEDGE'S PAST-LIFE

"Through the hole in this cake, I can see all of France."

"Merit is more common than pigs."

"People who believe in karma tend to be victims of it."

"As long as I don't love my food, it should be bearable."

"Plutocrats don't have as much money as me. They live in outer-space."

"My soul has more jewels than the king."

“What is uncommon to men is bane to the rule-makers. Quoting Machiavelli. The devil.”

“They ask me if I’m an evil dream?Well, that’s what I say when I make excuses! And I feel horrendous!”

“Without anxiety, I go to the window and admire Versailles. Sometimes I go to the roof. And ordinary view is not enough! It is like a museum, a museum of curious minds. Who pays the price? I feel like a financier! I have to remind the king to remember these words... Is the king God? This is a godawful place! There is lunacy even here, where the walls are paved with gold!”

“Everything small is a God—for it has not written a great big cheque... The woman’s place is to be God of the home... So I am spiritual like a woman... I am the God of Versailles... I rarely venture into the garden-forest... for there are smaller Gods that dwell there... Smaller Gods are more powerful Gods at Versailles... Versailles is the God of them all... And I am the smallest among Gods., and yet not a God at all... but a woman... A god of paradoxes.. The smallest of all Gods.. I am only a God at Versailles!”

1.

She was learning languages.

"What lesson do you have for me today?" said the teacher.

"Tempuesto, tempura, l' temps, Augusto, gest alto, agité," she repeated.

Sacristí, sacristiá, sacristé..." Then she trailed off.

"What is the word in Greek?" she asked.

"There is none." her teacher said. "But later, I have a secret."

Her father came to her. He said "You are to be the queen of France."

He said to her:

"You cannot go on speaking the wrong languages. You should speak only the real language of France"

"Apertur d' terre" she said.

"Apertur d' munde" he said.

"l' Munde, l' Munde, l' Munde" she repeated rebelliously (since the word didn't appear finished).

2.

It came time for the Queen of France to select a husband.

She spoke with her father.

"Who do you select to be you husband?" he asked

"Est un miscelle" she replied. "Au dressier 'Q'est bon heur' "

"N'est bon temps" he replied.

"Tromp l' temps au Msr. Dressier. Tromp l' heur. C'est bon temps"

3.

Finally she negotiated to leave her residence.

A kind gentleman navigated her to what seemed like the only three-story residence in all of France.

He said "It has three floors".

The trappings on the first floor were kind of posh.

"We're going to the third floor" he said.

"We can't go to the third floor, I'm deathly afraid of heights" she said.

"Don't distress. I'll dress you as a figurehead" he said.

She wasn't quite sure what this meant, but it sounded fancy. She felt suddenly the pull of a commitment---to this new thing.

He told her to undress, and she did, daintily she thought.

He told her to close her eyes, and when she opened them she would have a view of the city.

She was resting against some big satisfying thing.

Her breasts were pushed up by the force of the object.

He told her she would have a great wonderful feeling.

Then he entered her, and she had a great sensation of joy.
In the guise of a figurehead, she had many an ecstasy.

Only he hadn't properly introduced himself, so she didn't think of the man behind her.

She imagined her blood dripping and oozing onto all of France.

Later she remembered it as the only three-story building in all of France.

4.

"This isn't lettuce. It's garbage"

The new king said: "That's what she thinks of the lettuce. That it's garbage. She thinks it's not fit to eat. You know, I think she thinks I know how to fuck. But I don't. It's useless to fuck. Everyone I know that knows how to fuck has died. They've died fucking. Died!"

"What's the use?" the advisor replied. "She doesn't like the lettuce. She's sure not to like you in bed. You look like a mushroom, I understand. It's how everyone looks. No one who dislikes lettuce loves a mushroom. You can quote me on that in private" said the advisor.

"Next we'll be talking about apples and Eve! Good grief! She's not Eve. She's not even an Adam. I mean, look at her carriage. I mean, look at her rear end! It's hideous!" said the king.

"It's how they all look when they're down in the porridge" said the advisor, trying to make him more comfortable, and failing utterly. "She looks like my mother" he said. "If you'll pardon the pun".

"Good grief. Heaven fell on this such trippant mischief!" said the king. "What we need is poetry! What we need is a good vacation! Or better yet, a palace to vacation in! That would be love!"

"I know just the place, and it is Versailles!" she said.

"I haven't heard you say such a poetic thing in my entire life" said the king. "It may be the most poetic thing I've ever heard. But knowing you..." [gasp] "it will be your last...!"

"I hope you don't mean a beheading!" she said.

"Oh dear... That's the most ghastly thing I've every heard! Not a beheading. We're going to pomp some francs on a vacation palace, in Versailles. I hope to the lord that that isn't a pun."

"What a relief...and good grief" she said (in French).

“Ghastly...” he said.

“A ghastly palace named Versailles. Built in the sky with wings of brass. It turned into the image of pain. And then I died” she said. Romanticism was beginning to be in vogue, she thought.

“Ghastly poem... ghastly” he said. “And too English”.

“You noticed that” she said, in an English accent.

“Now you’re playing fair” he said. “You’ve changed a bit” he said, in an English accent, and in English.

“I have no reply to that” she said, in English, and in what she thought to be an American accent.

“That’s far afield. To Versailles we go! We’ll requisition the grounds!” he said.

“Joi d’ Vivre, if it’s not a pun” she said.

5.

“Chambre d’ amour d’ piscin?” she said.

“D’ piscin fragrance” he said.

"Dans l' mer d' si amour" she said.

"Nais c'est fabriqué" said the king.

They got under the covers.

"Sur nom vaginé. Dans le vaginé."

He mounted her, and then a foul look came across his face. "Putrifiqué!" he said.

"Poir Si Nomine Anglique?" she said. What if we call it the English?

"Nominé Latiné? C'est Angliqué! J'fusilée reine d' Francais!" I fire the Queen of France he said. Now you're my dirty mistress he said. This is getting more English by the minute he said.

"Dans le vaginé?" she repeated.

"Putrifiqué!" he said.

"Revellé?...Carcellé? Exposité?" she mused at him.

"Revellé l' reine d' Francais? Por sois? Bon! Dans le vaginé, putrifiqué! Mon Leib! Sur le bon, poesée! Putrifiquée poesée! Mon Leib!"

6.

The time in the palace seemed like forever.

The king arrived at a kind of moral in the mean-time:

“A woman has everything and gives it all away!
A king has a gift, and spends it thriftily”

This reasoning was golden. So she hoped to God.

7.

They were reading books together.

Their unluckiness had become a game.

“Abandon hope all ye who enter here” she said. “It should be written into all the Bibles”

“It will be like Babel.” said the king. “Who reads the whole thing?”

“It’s not a riddle.” she said. “I’ve invented Hell”.

Then she laughed as well as she could.

8.

“Madame Rege” someone said.

“This is musical!” she said. “Get some chairs! We’ll play music, and play with the chairs. Whoever wins, their heads will play the role.”

After some time… The king remained in the middle. Perhaps he had just stepped in.

“Were you playing?” he said. She joined him in the middle.

“I’m lucky” she said.

“This is the viscompte of Chardin” he replied. “He’s not to be trifled with”.

“I don’t care.” she said. “I’ve invented this, kind of like Hell”.

He turned red and wouldn’t say that she was mad.

9.

She was having time with her hair stylist.

“Shall I try to be master of the papers again?” she said. “You should instruct them to write certain things, like: 'she was least understood in her own terms' "

"I like it." he said. "Very *ordinaire*. Very cusp-of-the-times."

The newspaper ran with all the things she said, and it was a big success.

The queen of France was now also the Queen of fashion.

"Tromp l' temps." she said.

10.

She was saying to the king:

"Graci. Por l' 'mage. Terre terre rouge. Ignite l' chambre d' aur."

Later, he brought her flowers.

"Assure, S'bon. Ignite l' aur." he said.

"We aren't imbecilic art basels!" she said. "These flowers rot away!".

It was yet another sign of bad luck.

11.

"It was her folly to have nothing of what she had everything of" ---said of

Marie Antoinette

Reading the newspaper: "It's perfectly bad. It's so much who she IS," an advisor replied.

"You ruined it again. We're having a honeymoon" the king said.

"Another one?" The advisor said.

"The first one didn't work. It was perfectly bad. She's still perfectly bad, only she's so much more fair" he said.

"You're like the sun poet with her" he said.

"That was so much more beautiful than much of what she said" he said. "We'll make beautiful. We'll have the longest vacation. But I don't know if I'll recover"

"I'm sorry" the advisor said.

"Don't say sorry. Things are looking worse and worse for the French, I'm afraid".

"You're afraid?"

"No, she's afraid! She's a woman. He said. I'm beheaded! You know, I'm beheaded and disgruntled like a pig! This is getting more English by the minute!"

12.

Eventually her attention came to the library.

"You know Michel d' Montaigne?" the king asked.

"He's a man." she said.

"That's what I like" he said. "A woman who keeps her head in a cupboard".

She glanced at herself in one of the many mirrors that circled the great room.

"My nose is hideous. I have humor to thank that I'm a female and not a hermaphrodite" she said.

"You're not gay. You're not even a man!" he said. He said: "Soon I will show you something that must matter to your cold heart"

The room echoed with the sound of his beating heart. Or was it the guns fired by the soldiers?

13.

"Come and look at this" the king said. "It's a Cloissone egg. Only a few of them were made".

She began to believe in her own subjectivity. These were marvels, run by invisible machines, with gold grommets and inlayed intricatesse.

How mysterious! She thought. "I wonder if they contain a secret".

And the king, clucking, said "They certainly do. See if you can fish them out".

Later, when he wasn't looking, she busted a few of them on the floor, to see if they contained the secret of ambergris.

"Only money" he said. "We're not the gods of Olympus".

It was her great disillusionment. The mystery, however, seemed to remain real, even when the dust was swept away.

14.

She once said the king was "cold and

challenging".

She thought he would never forgive her.

But instead he loved her all the more.

15.

She was always wondering in response to other people.

She considered this to be metaphysical.

"If we eat food then it's like there are pigs"

At another time she said:

"Through this cake, I can see all of France".

16.

She remembers how she invented magical thread. She was sitting in the library studying Ariadne.

"We have extra thread. Let's sell it to the evil serfs" she said.

"It's not that they're evil, so much as that they're too good" the king said.

"So far as Ariadne goes, they have an evil inclination to sew their lips together" he said.

17.

The next night she had an insight at the stroke of midnight.

"Musical thread!" she said.

The next morning , they called for the most magical musician, and had him appear in court.

"Sheer-ah-ho-ah-sheer-ah-ho-ah,
Sheer-ah-ho-ah-sheer-ah heer"

He played. The king declared it to be enchanting.

"We can use the musician to sell the thread" she said.

18.

At first the thread was a tough sell. No one seemed to be able to market the material.

"Situate him in a high room nearby" she said. She was speaking of the musician.

19.

The thread was selling well, and they began to get greedy.

“What will make these serfs buy more thread?” The king said

“We need to get a special salesperson, a certain really good sales person” the queen said.

20.

It took some time, but soon the vizier reported that a new salesperson had been found.

“Indeed, he sells ten times the amount of thread. It’s a miracle” he said.

“Pay him 15 Francs an hour” she said.

“How much does he make?” she asked.

“Oh, well near 1500” he replied.

“Keep him on 15 and collect money by the hour” she said.

“How much shall we pay the musician?”

“Pay him 5 Francs to keep him bleak” she said.

21.

Next news:

"The musician has quit. He's demanding more Francs." said the Vizier.

"Pay him 17 Francs an hour, and make sure it's fair" she said.

Then he reported back: "He's taken 17 as a sign to quit, because it means temperance."

"Pay him another 17 and tell him he's to be temperate with being temperate" she said.

Then he reported back: "The musician has played himself to death".

She never heard the real story because all of France was in chaos.

22.

One crazy day, "Requiré societé clandestín" said the king.

"Societé clandestín? Por sois?" she said.

"J'nais pas requiré. Requiré francs" he was saying.

23.

One terrible winter, the palace was frozen.

The king and the queen huddled by the fireplace.

“This is the end of the affair of crepes Suzette” the king was saying.

He was removing the burnt remains of their attempt at cooking.

The servants were nowhere to be found.

She would never forget the image of burning Francs in her mind.

“Let’s go get warm together” said the King.

“ S’ oi” she said.

They took off their clothes, under the covers, as best they could.

“We look so different in our other selves” she said.

“You know, this is how we look, how we naturally are” he said.

It seemed like a statement of natural philosophy.

Philosophers seemed so cold in this domineering weather.

24.

One day, revolutionaries arrived at the palace.

They asked her to "Come in their company."

She thought the revolution was over.

They looked just like any other soldiers to her.

Then one of them shouted "That's the wealth that she gives us, the bitch".

"That's a fine thing to say in a house like this" she said.

There were mutters of contempt.

She realized the war had not ended her way.

25...

Commenting before her death, she remarked "Maybe she was more brilliant than I remember". She thought she had sold her soul in that moment.

She was talking with a gawker, saying "It's all made of cloth, the king has said so himself. I have no rear end," when she realized she had missed the beheading of the king.

There was an angry mob. Someone shouted in the crowd "Name no one man!"

She swore under her breath "Damned with the dram". Then she shouted back "Perhaps it's that the king has fleas. You can name this 'pallendrome' after me! It's called a pallendrome, in my honor, she said."

"Did you really say that we should eat cake?" someone shouted.

"I said if you look through cake it is a window onto France" she said.

"It's just an experience" she would have said, but her voice was drowned out by the crowd.

"Are you a revolutionary?" someone said.

"My love is for the king" she replied.

"The king's francs?" someone shouted angrily.

"Devil!" someone said.

"Murder her!" someone screamed.

She was asked to summarize her life. "I thought it was practical" she said.

Then she had a glimpse of the world swirling, bouncing, and turning dim.

Life was gone like a bleeding scarf, she thought, in her decapitated head.

26...

Circa 2005

Someone approaches Nathan Coppedge. They are wearing a small microphone, like a secret service agent.

"Someone tells me that you were Marie Antoinette"

"Maybe...I don't quite remember" I reply.

"Yes...I've found her." he says in his microphone. "She has whiskers. And she's gone batty. She has ears..."

“Okay!” I can hear someone saying on the other end.

“Should I requisition her or what?” he says.

A dimly muffled voice replies.

Then he asks me: “Are you rich?”

I say: “No, I’m poor. I’m not sure that I have any money.”

“Case solved!” I can hear him saying.

And then trailing into the distance: “Thank God!”

I can almost feel him disappearing like a Djinn. But I’m too scared to look.

27...

Recounting my life as Marie Antoinette, I tried to re-phrase my attitudes towards life and death.

“It occurs to me that I have never drunk wine” I say.

“Now the price of opulence is perpetual motion. That or world peace.” I inquire.

I pose a question to myself: "Would perpetual motion cause world peace?"

And I answer in her voice: "Possibly. It should, but it might not".

"The world seems to depend on my divinity, since everyone else has been drinking wine, and I call for world peace or something that would make everyone rich as the king of France. Barring that, solitude is what is called for. And I suspect it is not just my subjectivity."

NATHAN COPPEDGE

Billing himself as a philosopher, artist, inventor, and poet, Nathan promotes himself mostly online. However, his ambitions are archaic: building perpetual motion machines, writing neo-classical literature, making sublime poems. He also makes modern art! In school, he excels, until he develops madness while attending college in New York State during the September 11th attacks. While still attending school in New Haven for a philosophy degree, he writes numerous books and quotations, creates hundreds of art works, and think he has found the secret of perpetual motion---even if he can't build it himself.

QUOTATIONS BY NATHAN COPPEDGE

"Metaphor is the ladder to higher systems" ---Nathan Coppedge, Nov 2014.

"Categories are the standard of standardization"

---Deceptively genius quote by Nathan

Coppedge as posted on Twitter in March 2014, blog in mid to late 2013.

"While they (other inventors) were floundering, he was pondering / 'No more wandering through the dark tunnels of grim determination / For no; it is time to grow in a thousand folded folds / For which we need an infinite fuel (such as perpetual motion)"

---Nathan Coppedge, circa 2009

"The ideal aperture (to philosophy) is with miscellany"

This is perceived as the core of the Dimensional Philosopher's Toolkit, by Nathan Coppedge.

"The outer universe might be the inner universe, and the inner universe might be the outer universe, and there is nothing dividing these things. Either there is continuity or there is not, and in either case the universe is continuous or it isn't. Either case is expressed as an objective philosophical fact."

--- Nathan Coppedge, Nov 2014

"Two locations require a common application, and two applications require a common location. Apparently, there is continuity or there is not"

--- Nathan Coppedge, Nov 2014

"I'm tempted to think that sadism is an economic problem, in the larger sense of the word"

--- Nathan Coppedge (2014) .

"The world is clockwork in the distance."

--- Nathan Coppedge,2014

"Matter is meaning, in whatever form it takes"

--- Nathan Coppedge,2014

"Because I am looking for a system that does not lack qualities..."

--- Nathan Coppedge, from 6 Theories of Metaphysics

"Life needs a subject, so it needs an intermedium."

--- Nathan Coppedge, from 6 Theories of Metaphysics

"An artist is the subject of life. Consequently, life can be designed."

--- Nathan Coppedge,2014 (cited in 6 Theories of Metaphysics) .

"Context is a fulfillment application."

--- Nathan Coppedge,2014 (cited in 6 Theories of Metaphysics) .

"Objective knowledge is like math with qualities."

--- Nathan Coppedge (2014) .

"It's the deadest thing to say. But my form of inspiration is mechanical."

--- Nathan Coppedge (2014) .

"Some would compare intelligence to a miracle the way I compare a fortune to madness."--- Nathan Coppedge (2014) .

"Time is a material abstractification."

- Nathan Coppedge (2013) .

"There are higher forms of madness like there are higher forms of silver."

--- Nathan Coppedge (2014) .

"If there is no volition, it is a failure of dimension, if not perspective. I'm led to believe that one of the categories of volition is abstraction (I don't mean pejoratively. That is, insofar as abstraction doesn't have to be a game) ."
--- Nathan Coppedge (2014) .

"Time travel is possible in any exceptional-conditional reality of that type."

--- Nathan Coppedge

"Problematics does not provide ultimate solutions."

--- Nathan Coppedge

"[W]hat is necessary... is finding relevance for the development within the formalism."

--- Nathan Coppedge, in an article called Introduction to Formal Technicalism.

"[New Formalism may be applied to business in five steps:] A. What is the formalism? B. How to apply it? C. What is the big idea? D. What is the context? E. What is the epiphany?"

--- Nathan Coppedge, in an article titled Introduction to Formal Technicalism.

"(In philosophy and mathematics,) Nothing is formal everything."

--- Nathan Coppedge (objective typology pyramid, for a book on metaphysics) .

"Form is (inherently) coherent. What is incoherent is coherently incoherent. I find this to be a rule of nature."

- Nathan Coppedge (2014) .

"Realities are immunities."

---Nathan Coppedge (first law of the fourth dimension) .

"Problems are isomorphized."

---Nathan Coppedge, (2nd law of the fourth dimension) .

"Problems are not global."

---Nathan Coppedge (3rd law of the fourth dimension) .

"Ideals are not idealizations."

---Nathan Coppedge (4th law of the fourth dimension) .

"There are objective qualities and mathematical anomalies."

--- Nathan Coppedge, 'the Third Soul of the Dimensional Encyclopedia'.

"I am a citizen of an unknown place. I wonder where it belongs?"

--- Nathan Coppedge, 'The 2nd Soul of the Dimensional Encyclopedia'.

"The concept is an endless ladder."

--- Nathan Coppedge, 'The First Soul of the Dimensional Encyclopedia'.

"Preservation is very easy now, so the focus should be on pure ideas. Some realize this, but at the same time, few have realized it in their art... [M]any have opted to be stonewalled by the relationship between meaning and representation."

--- Nathan Coppedge, comment at the Abstract Art group on LinkedIn (December 2014) .

"I am the most specialized of pure generalists that I know. More abstract would be more extreme, but it would also be more empty."

--- Nathan Coppedge (2013) .

"I found a system without math!"

--- Nathan Coppedge (2013)

"Representational reality is virtual reality."

--- Nathan Coppedge

"Preferring subjectivity over death is still absolutism."

--- Nathan Coppedge (2014) .

"[C]ompleteness. It was the most outrageous fact - - the kind of fact some authors have mistaken for death."

--- Nathan Coppedge (The Techne,2014)

"Somewhere beyond the exercise of the imagination...was an outer boundary...Every question appertained to it."

--- Nathan Coppedge (The Techne,2014) .

"The symbol of everything belonged anywhere."

--- Nathan Coppedge (The Techne,2014) .

"Metaphysics granted me that all were variables."

--- Nathan Coppedge (The Techne,2014).

"Practical advice was the domain of a scripted set of perfections."

--- Nathan Coppedge (The Techne,2014) .

"Imagination could live there if it's whole point was not to be dangerous. But the merest hint of adventure, and the mind would snap, and the subject would not longer be practical."

--- Nathan Coppedge, On practicality (The Techne,2014) .

"Not only practicality was perfect."

--- Nathan Coppedge (The Techne,2014) .

"Nihilism was the conviction that a person was no more than a value."

--- Nathan Coppedge (The Techne,2014) .

"Successful religions are subtle annihilations- -the apocrypha of nihilists... Successful people use value as neutral currency, in this sense becoming profoundly immoral."

--- Nathan Coppedge (The Techne,2014) .

"Imagination can be a force of politics

when it is seen that it is imagination doing the computation."

--- Nathan Coppedge (The Techne,2014) .

"Perhaps, I thought, I was having an absurd religious experience."

--- Nathan Coppedge (The Techne,2014) .

"[I]t was a representation, so it was a polytheism."

--- Nathan Coppedge (The Techne,2014) .

"I was now a politician of the meaningless. The sort of person who has meaningful things to say..."

--- Nathan Coppedge (The Techne,2014) .

"And sometimes EVERYTHING is what

people need..."

--- Nathan Coppedge (The Techne,2014) .

"The sages are full of advice about doing nothing. It is often better than doing the wrong thing."

--- Nathan Coppedge (The Techne,2014) .

"[W]hen I think of the practical, I think of returning to EVERYTHING..."

--- Nathan Coppedge (The Techne,2014) .

"We can't get everything merely by being practical, and hence, we can't get practicality merely from being practical."

--- Nathan Coppedge (The Techne,2014) .

"Practicality is inevitably a simplification."

--- Nathan Coppedge (The Techne,2014) .

"If the task is difficult and ordinary, then chances are, there is someone who can say that it involves a 'special technique'. If there is no special technique available, it is either sacred knowledge, or you're supposed to delegate the task to someone else. If you cannot delegate, and you don't think it's sacred knowledge, and it doesn't involve a special technique, then you know that Fate will step in, for better or worse."

--- Nathan Coppedge (The Techne,2014) .

"To avoid mediocrity, it is important to delegate."

--- Nathan Coppedge (The Techne,2014) .

"[O]nly the trickiest, most intelligent people seem self-sufficient...They have learned to depend on other people's minds instead of their bodies. They have raised the standard, and climbed on top of other people's backs. Only by being dependent have they begun to look independent."

--- Nathan Coppedge, (The Techne,2014) .

"[Concerning the higher life...] it is partly because they're delegating about their fate, and their sacred knowledge is a special technique."

--- Nathan Coppedge (The Techne,2014) .

"There is no rule which says that the universe is more complex than we are."

--- Nathan Coppedge (Dec 2014) .

"All that I saw missing in previous criticism was an actual system of criticism: so I provided one."

--- Nathan Coppedge (January 2015) .

"Questioning the legitimacy of language is like questioning the legitimacy of opposites."

--- Nathan Coppedge (January 2015) .

"Genius SUBJECTIVELY is not the way to design a perpetual motion machine."

--- Nathan Coppedge, Jan 2015.

"Sometimes I, more than others, define my own context of criticism."

--- Nathan Coppedge, Jan 2015.

"Sometimes I determine that I don't have access to reality. Then I can determine: at least I don't feel depressed."

--- Nathan Coppedge, Jan 2015.

"If I've learned one thing from my relative fame it's that actors are brilliant tacticians."

--- Nathan Coppedge, Jan 2015.

"Real technology is metaphysical."

---Nathan Coppedge (2014) .

"Success is knowing you have good things to talk about."

---Nathan Coppedge (Around 2013 - 2015) .

"Art is the metaphysics of philosophy."

---Nathan Coppedge (2014,2015) .

"'The concept of value abolishes ultimatums'."

---Nathan Coppedge (Yahoo Answers, January 19th,2015)

"Sane people are enumerators of challenges. On this basis, they can be understood to the mad."

---Nathan Coppedge (Jan.31st,2015)

"Neutrality is like perfect judgment."

---Nathan Coppedge (February 2015) .

"Some poets have said that poets are thieves only because they are historically illiterate. In reality, many things are illiterate, and few things belong to anyone except through the coincidence of their opinion."

---Nathan Coppedge, (February 2015) .

"If we don't grant ourselves the right exceptions, we won't achieve immortality."

---Nathan Coppedge (February 2015) .

"Paroxysms tend to be solutions because we focus on the problems. Otherwise they might seem like ordinary paradoxes. But don't be mistaken. If a paradox cannot be solved by paroxysm, it is already a solution."

---Nathan Coppedge, (February 2015) .

"Micro socialism is like totalitarianism without violence."

---Nathan Coppedge (February 2015) .

"Maximize technicalism and you maximize frustration. No technicalism is maximal. Because of the balance of functions, intermediates are preferred."

---Nathan Coppedge, (February 2015) .

"Determinism is God's opinion about

the depressed."

---Nathan Coppedge (March,2015) .

"Stupidity is basically our inability to grasp the meaningless. It is marked by an indecision about arbitrary meanings. Stupidity is indecisive and concerns itself with superficial explanations."

---Nathan Coppedge (March 2015) .

"(Vis. immortal evolution) , the questions, as well as the answers, will change..."

---Nathan Coppedge (March 2015) .

"[R]elative adaptation depends on the informational structure of the world. And, in an age other than information, it reflects other paradigms..."

---Nathan Coppedge (March 2015) .

"[A]n ancient proverb says that age is wisdom. But there are different kinds of age..."

---Nathan Coppedge (March 2015) . Based on extensive articles on the subject of immortality, published as a book titled The Secret Principles of Immortality (Vol I) .

"The current state of the world is always an attempt to find the best explanation."

---Nathan Coppedge, (March 2015) .

"The only thing without meaning is the economy of meaning"

---Nathan Coppedge, to be published in the Spiritual Writings and Dimensional Phenomenologist's Toolkit Appendix I, Part 2.

"Coherence does not necessitate many worlds."

---Nathan Coppedge, 'Implications of Dimensional Knowledge'.

"Exceptions must be technical."

---Nathan Coppedge, 'Implications of Dimensional Knowledge'.

"Each of the cases illustrates a certain exceptionalism. They are restricted cases sort of like a solar-powered computer, or bubbles suspended in the process of carbonation."

---Nathan Coppedge, 'Super-Finite Engineering'.

"Transformation (technicalism) occurs through similar states, neutral states, and opposite states."

---Nathan Coppedge, 'Implications of Dimensional Knowledge'.

"Opposite states usually exist for separate reasons...Otherwise, opposite states arise through neutrals."

---Nathan Coppedge, 'Implications of Dimensional Knowledge'.

"Perhaps the mad are the ones that really receive the message, only because it is, for them, urgent information- - a matter of jealousy."

---Nathan Coppedge, 'The Voki' (in The Dimensional Phenomenologist's Toolkit) .

"Whether they are mad or religious or politicians, the message they receive is that they are in a city, and they hear the messages that concern city-dwellers."

---Nathan Coppedge, 'The Voki' (in The Dimensional Phenomenologist's Toolkit) .

"The Insistent Instant of light- - something more real than light which is merely found."

---Nathan Coppedge, to be published in the Spiritual Writings and Dimensional Phenomenologist's Toolkit Appendix I, Part 2.

"Nothingness. The way of self-adaptation."

---Nathan Coppedge, to be published in the Spiritual Writings and Dimensional Phenomenologist's Toolkit Appendix I, Part 2.

"So either consciousness is an outlier, or people always get what they want, or there is no way to explain pain, because pain cannot be explained if it is not what someone wants....To be sane, the individual has to align with the majority, which involves explaining pain away, or leaving it unexplained. But the self-examined life leads to the rejection of these views."

---Nathan Coppedge, Scientific Theories

"(According to the method of paroxysm) , human folly is ultimately solved by inhuman wisdom."

---Nathan Coppedge, 'Work on Truth and Philosophical Irrationality Vis. Absolutism'.

"It is hard to prove something impossible that is partly possible."

---Nathan Coppedge, blog (April 8th,2015) .

"Some forms of art may even remember the future."

---Nathan Coppedge,2015.

"Sometimes the best thing for fools is horrible for the intelligence of children."

---Nathan Coppedge,2015.

"The most flattering recognitions are a vanity of the times."

---Nathan Coppedge,2015.

"The word inhuman is the primary supporter of capital punishment."

---Nathan Coppedge,2015

"Materialism is a metaphor far deeper than physics."

---Nathan Coppedge (May 2015) .

"Darwinism, Economics, Meaning... Meaning is two degrees of difficulty beyond Darwinism."

---Nathan Coppedge

"Where there is not sufficient meaning, there is a mysterious purpose."

---Nathan Coppedge, 'Experiential Metaphysics', in The Dimensional

Metaphysics Toolkit (unpublished work) .

"Scientist, logician, poet, artist... If your pleasure is good for others, then you will thrive, even if you are not those things. (But those are the fundamental forms of rationality)."

---Nathan Coppedge

"Where some things have material conditions, there are also immaterial conditions which potentially exist. These outer conditions, whether they are material or not, may be called design."

---Excerpted Note, Nathan Coppedge

"Meaningful information need not obey the laws of time."

---Nathan Coppedge

"Truth may be, in itself, the obviation

of the obvious."

---Nathan Coppedge

"And, as for space-time, it is clear that space-time...is simply a compounding of opportunities..."

---Nathan Coppedge, 'Pre-Delineation of Time as Opportunism', in The Dimensional Phenomenologist's Toolkit.

"Do small things to improve your health incrementally as time goes on. By this logic, if you are infinitely old, you will definitely be infinitely healthy!"

---Nathan Coppedge (Nathan's Techniques for Immortality,2015).

"By your own definition, try to be lucid about your entire life whenever possible. This involves seeing through the mists of time that enshroud your life, and making some predictions about what will happen to you, and what your life means. This will make you relatively wise compared to people who do not do this."

---Nathan Coppedge, ('Nathan's Techniques for Immortality', short article published 2015).

"See your own past as something that was infinitely old, and your future as something moderately young. This will allow you to justify endless good health. Life is not a sacrifice or something idiotic, but rather an endless struggle to regain lost wisdom, by becoming young."

---Nathan Coppedge, (Nathan Coppedge's Techniques for Immortality, short article published 2015) .

"Make little bets with yourself about what something means. It could be whether you look at a car passing, or whether you choose to smile or eat a snack at a given moment. If it turns out one way, you decide that it has a given result. So you use it to hone your willpower. Not only that, but you use it to gain motivation about what you can really achieve. You can tell yourself, ‘my smile means immortality' or ‘when I eat this snack, it's for a good reason, so I'm going to make some achievement'. Instead of being completely flexible, apply principle now and then, and use it as guidance for the long-term."

---Nathan Coppedge, (Nathan's Techniques for Immortality, short article published 2015) .

"In effect, an idea is the opinion of God. What is real for us is some holy genius' idea. The idea in our minds is someone's second-hand opinion. Yet, what is real is real. Choices divide the access to the best reality."

---Nathan Coppedge, The Dimensional Phenomenologist's Toolkit.

"What matters is not only the object, but also the meaning of the object. While this seems like a cop-out, in fact it is a subtler answer than phenomenal intensionality. We can attribute objectivity to causality and formative principles, as well as our own pragmatic purposes- -or forms of critique- -rather than reducing an object into a supposedly objective viewpoint which is only an interpretation."

---Nathan Coppedge, June 2015.

"We can blame the supposed lack of an original object upon the process of having a meaningful interpretation. For there is no rule which says that the object's causes must have meaning. And, although the human mind is capable of ascribing causes to an object, it is not always capable of ascribing meaningful causation. The same is not true of interpretation. And that is why original objects are seen to be meaningless. Yet, if they were meaningful, we would believe in them, only we would likely hold them to be contingent upon some process of critique. But the process of critique is really a way of involving ourselves in the process of finding meaning, e.g. from the sources of things in causal and acausal laws. If the original object seems meaningless, since it may arise from meaningless causes, this says nothing against the reality of the original object."

---Nathan Coppedge, June 2015.

"We find causation meaningless, so objects are real! Of course! Even if they participate with our minds, that doesn't mean that the objects or the mind have to be absolute! Nor does it guarantee that we don't have a mind. To prove a mind does not require proving a complete mind, for according to relativity, any kind of mind is, in some way, a mind. Therefore, whatever has an opinion that it is a mind, is in some way, officially, a mind. For any sort of mind is capable of meaningful translation, even if the perspective that translates is not the original mind. The mind itself is a kind of object, even if there is no standard to objectify it. The absence of standards is never reason enough to prove that something is without reality."

---Nathan Coppedge, June 2015.

"Basically, there's some variable that's killing me. Am I dying of democracy? Do immortals ask this question? Should I know everything?"

---Nathan Coppedge, June 2015.

"The devil could convince you that he is a saint. But he wouldn't call himself a devil, would he? Then I would be like him! And how is it just not about me? But that would be a real trick. It couldn't be a trick if the devil had tricked you. So I did trick you, but I didn't really. Therefore, I'm a saint and not the devil."

---Nathan Coppedge, June 2015.

"When your meaning is cursed, that's when your life is cursed; when your meaning is blessed, that's when your life is blessed. Fortunately, meaning is a creative act: we can thrive not only on affirmative objects, but on the potential to uncover future meanings."

---Nathan Coppedge, June 2015.

"Someone said that pragmatic virtue seems to include all of the sins. That is, whereas virte (strong virtue) may happen to obey idealizations: from this I get the idea that idealizations are virtue in a meaningful way, if we consider the whole society."

---Nathan Coppedge, June 2015.

"Predicting demand or predicting product deflation become the rudimentary tools, apart from GDP and investor confidence, unless the goal is to predict the success of a specific company within the market."

---Nathan Coppedge, The Dimensional Economics Toolkit.

"Throw a bunch of fools at eachother: that's exactly how war is fought! Declare the method and the reason will out! Declare the reason, and the methods will change! If they change indefinitely, there will be no more war."

---Nathan Coppedge, July 2015.

"Biology should really be some other concept, just like psychology should be some other concept. At least according to views of the ideal universe. This is what I conclude from the ideal, yet almost failed delineation of the volumes of my encyclopedia."

---Nathan Coppedge, July 2015.

"Psychology is the first resort when philosophy is compromised. It reaches interesting theories."

---Nathan Coppedge, July 2015.

"It takes infinite variables to create an infinite universe. And when it comes down to it, some variables are not mere variables, but qualities, modes, and systems."

---Nathan Coppedge, July 2015.

"[On social theories:] I think it's a systemic failure. But the system is improving. People have been passing away too frequently to know that it improves. Recent psychology valued confidence and took improvement for granted. The result was pessimism."

---Nathan Coppedge, July 2015.

"I think different people have different needs. If they have the same needs, then they can be met by mass production."

---Nathan Coppedge, July 2015.

"A functional society can be provided resources easily with mass production. Where there is demand for services, because of robotics, there is demand for creative potential. Where there is no demand for services, then there is a guarantee that needs can be met. Therefore, whether or not there is a demand for services, there is some capacity to meet the need."

---Nathan Coppedge, July 2015.

"Economics is... the capacity to buy into meaning, and then create it cheaply, and improve it when excess funds are available."

---Nathan Coppedge, blog comment on political views, July 2015.

"[I]mmortal athletes are prophets, not daredevils."

---Nathan Coppedge, from The Dimensional Immortality Toolkit. Nathan sometimes also speaks against athleticism.

"Tautological incompleteness is actually inadequate against relative proof. Nor does theory need to prove the tautological."

---Nathan Coppedge, July 2015. Following an attempt to refute Godel's Incompleteness.

"The entities that determine power will find laws are futile that do not take heed of significance. Perhaps not even ultimately, but in some way one must make sacrifices if one does not serve the significance of life. Therefore, what scares me is that there are several ultimate models which create psychological and political strife: these are the lawful, the rich, the meaningless, and the desperate. (Meaninglessness is a choice, and desperation is not a mode of functionality, but there you have it: the dangers of life laid bare in terms of significance)."

---Nathan Coppedge, July 2015.

"Perfectionism is the typical missing link for the history of dialectical critique, and ignoring it brings grave dangers of circuity."

---Nathan Coppedge, 'Genius Correspondences'.

"The blindness of God is merely the absence of a spiritual dimension of existence, which can be determined arbitrarily by the mere choice to pertain or not to pertain to the higher dimensions."

---Nathan Coppedge, 'Genius Correspondences'.

"Where politics does not realize paradise, artificial answers will continue to impinge."

---Nathan Coppedge, 'Genius Correspondences'. Also will be included in a project called Prophetic Wisdom.

"The bounded Cartesian Coordinate System relates to Einstein's relativity... [T]hat does not appear to reduce it to randomness - - but rather, democritization."

---Nathan Coppedge, 'Genius Correspondences'.

"I don't claim to have written a lot, I have just claim to have written a lot of books."

---Nathan Coppedge, July 2015.

"A chain-of-events that makes a subject out of experience is still an objective application, where the experience consists of objects."

---Nathan Coppedge, July 2015.

"In my experience, success is always about universalism."

---Nathan Coppedge, July 2015.

"Nothing is meaningless to the perpetual traveler."

---Nathan Coppedge

"The formula of the known is not the same as the identity for change, although sometimes they swap operators while living amongst statues."

---Nathan Coppedge, July 2015. Related to higher-order logic.

"Identity, it strikes me, is to a huge degree an open-ended concept. There is nothing about identity which says that it does not oppose itself, or that it did not adopt some difficult obscurity for its realization. From this type of principle I arrive at the idea that identity is universally exceptional."

---Nathan Coppedge, The Dimensional Politics Toolkit, (also included in Nathan Coppedge's Scientific Theories) .

" 'What occurs when the symbolic boundary is crossed diagonally? ' I have asked this question again and again, and the answer largely appears to be the emergence of a new system. While in other conceptualizations the result would be failure, I see no reason to believe that the other attempters gave any consideration to the just criteria."

---Nathan Coppedge, The Dimensional Metaphysics Toolkit

"Things like language proliferate, and with them, a wide variety of logics- - or other, far more obscure terms. If we are too enmettled to realize this, at least it serves the value of our complexity."

---Nathan Coppedge, The Dimensional Subjectivity Toolkit. Duplicated in The Dimensional Anthropology Toolkit. Attributed to Posterity, a goddess.

"Concerning universal anthropology: To the dimensional sense of the person, the central motif appears to be satisfaction, or some variation on it. Species that do not develop satisfaction are purely logical, and easily manipulated."

---Nathan Coppedge, The Dimensional

Anthropology Toolkit

"'To trace the exact path, amongst so many promises, has a twinge of the animal. Until the hypothetical researcher realizes that the process concerns the immortal, the animal will be concerned with the researcher, without knowing she exists.'"

---Nathan Coppedge, July 2015.

"One can devote oneself to the most basic, most primitive concepts of working tools, but this denies the future of evolution...At one point I may have determined that this meant selling my soul. But now it means that primitive tools require advanced conceptualizations in an advanced world..."

---Nathan Coppedge, The Basic Book.

"You could say economics is the evolution of evolution. And meaning is the evolution of economics. But whether we reach each of these stages depends on the exact circumstances that prefigure their possibility. In this way, meaning is still evolution, and economics is still survival."

---Nathan Coppedge, July to August 2015.

"Criticism ends with an artistic choice... It is tempting to say that it is only this sense in which art is mad... Even when people consider other distinctions, there is nothing about the process that is not either exceptional or desperate... And evolution itself evinces desperation..."

---Nathan Coppedge, August 2015.

"Mathematical incoherency might be solvable by referring to something non-mathematical."

---Nathan Coppedge, The Solutions, August 2015.

"Because there is no innate unique thing separating the arbitrariness of one body from the arbitrariness of another body, so too, there is no innate unique sense of experience. Hence, there is no innate sense of Solipsism. You may not experience someone else's body- -but in a way you already are!"

---Nathan Coppedge, The Solutions, August 2015.

"[T]here is potentially no relation between free will and determinism. Free will represents the authentic sense of changeable objects, whereas determinism is a sense of changeless objects, of varying ambiguity."

---Nathan Coppedge, The Solutions, August 2015.

"Preferences are the maximal requirement for the will."

---Nathan Coppedge, The Solutions,
August 2015.

R.V. WINKL

MOST OF HIS MEANINGFUL WORDS

"I fell asleep for a 'hundred years. And I saw all kinds of strange men"

"Really? Strange men, huh? That's some story! A hundred years! I don't know if I believe that one. Say, come here and tell your story. Maybe I can git you a drink or some chub cuttling"

R.V. Winkl, squatting on a chair: "I saw strange men. And I fell asleep for a hundred years. That's it".

"Ha, ha!" someone said back to him. "I know some local actors that could pick up that bit! You'll be famous in no time!"

R.V. Winkl just smiled back at them. Then he said "I'm real ambitious. That's all I know".

Later the man came back, and there were all kinds of cheers, and some actors put on an unbelievable show that was half mischief and half the real thing.

He said "You say you're ambitious. You

should come talk with the you-know, real ambitious men folk out at the fire".

All the men tried to do at first was make him sit in the fire. But he knew better than that.

"I'll sit like a sage and wise man over here as I please" he said.

"Then we know you're a real man!" they said. "You're welcome among us!".

They were kind enough to give him food, but he didn't know what was in it. It didn't taste like the grittle at the kettle. Burnt he guessed. But it was delicious through and through.

Then talk came around to everyone's wants and ambitions.

One man wanted a wife, but the other man frowned on him, and said it wasn't wise. They said R.V. Winkl knows more than you, and he felt really good about it.

"Say, what do you want to be, Mr. R.V. Winkl, when you're on your feet so to speak, since you just got into this here town? When you become prosperous, I mean?"

R.V. Winkl got up from his stoop, then said nothing.

“Oh, you don’t have to be so formal and proper” they said. So he sat back down.

He thought about it, and they gave him a little more time. After a long while he said:

“I’m a real thinking man’s man. I want to be a kind of eschatologisticianist. I want to be rich, too”

“Well, you can’t be a rich man being a scatologo-ist” said someone. All they do is examine people’s ass, like this! He said, and he dropped his pants and gave everyone an eyeful.

“I don’t think that’s what I mean.“ R.V Winkl said. “What do those folks do who read books and look at pictures?” he said. “Like a priest, only more proper”

“Oh,” someone said. “You want to be like a Rabbi or a philo-logist. But that’s for Jewish folks”

“I want to be an esystemen-to-logist. I said what I meant and I meant what I said.”

“And it doesn‘t mean staring into nobody‘s A-hole” someone added.

After that, R.V. Winkl felt more justified.

(“Well, too late, and time for bed” the guy replied. Everyone looked at the statement like it wasn’t a rude awakening).

OTHER QUOTATIONS BY R.V. WINKL.

“Everyone spends too much for smokes. I don’t smoke. I have wrinkles enough. You can ask the local actors. They know who I am. Some of them have wrinkles enough, that’s what they said about me and not them. If I‘m so impudent, why don‘t I smoke too much tobacco?”

“Liquor is a heinous crime. It makes me feel ill. It has properties mal. It doesn’t pay the bills. Vote down the liquor arrangement. Hang the thieves that put up poster girls and medicine wives. End the peril of extradition to the devil. Get our money back on track. Back to basics, no more sick arrangements. Liquor is a wedding with the devil. It‘s not as practical as baking bricks. And you know back pain and then some when you try to lay a load of those ones. Vote R.V. Winkl for town doctor. He knows the liquor is terrible, and matters are getting worse for your lady-friends"

"I won't fight in this war. I won't ever. It's brother fighting brother. We don't even have weapons to fight. Without weapons, we're goners. Look at this crappy sword. It bends under my weight. It's fate: we're going to die or be saved"

SAINT DEVIL

“After discovering God he discovered a system,
After discovering a system he discovered perfection;
After discovering perfection he discovered volition;
After discovering volition he discovered eternity;
After discovering eternity he discovered geometry;
After discovering geometry he discovered synergy;
So wrote the devil” ---Saint Devil / On Death

“The guilty have to thank the liars,
The liars have to thank the gimmicks,
The gimmicks have to thank the evils,
So wrote the devil” ---Saint Devil / On Deafness

"A friend of mine is convinced he's not a devil. Anyone who has a friend like this is a devil himself."

--- Saint Devil, Jan 2015.

"If I tell the truth and you beg me to lie, then I earn the name saint devil. But, besuiting the name, it is a devilish course to be a devil: all that's left of the title is the name."

--- Saint Devil, Jan 2015.

"If people say I can't earn the name saint devil, I will tell them they can't prove that history is infallible, and besides, simply using name doesn't make it true! When is a name magical, and since when is THAT the basis for truth?"

--- Saint Devil, Jan 2015.

"When saint devil is a child he sounds like a pope."

--- Saint Devil, Jan 2015.

"Saint devil is a serious case of Babel. It's one of the only things that scares people."

--- Saint Devil, Jan 2015.

"Saint devil harvests meaninglessness in favor of fearful significance."

--- Saint Devil, Jan 2015.

"Translators are mistaken for interpreters: you need to be like saint devil to realize this."

--- Saint Devil, Jan 2015.

"His strangely lopsided hand was written before it was written."

--- Saint Devil, Jan 2015.

"They don't think devils are superficial: that's what saint devil can say."

--- Saint Devil, Jan 2015.

"The only thing more devilish than being saint devil is proving it. When history learns this, however, there won't be any devils."

--- Saint Devil, Jan 2015.

"I'm a bad painter when I'm a good devil."

--- Saint Devil, Jan 2015.

"If I want to be a creative devil, I think back to when I was an imp. When I was an imp, I took an I.M.P. math class and learned that history is evilly incomplete and incompletely evil. When I solved this problem, I solved the problem of the devil."

--- Saint Devil, Jan 2015.

"I'm not really saint devil. That would turn life into a living hell (for me) . But if I'm a liar or the devil, I may as well be a devil (I saw this to be sound reasoning)."

---Saint Devil (April 2015).

"Sometimes I think paradox is a more advanced concept than religion."

---Saint Devil, (May 2015).

"Picasso was God. And I'm saint devil. Saint devil has good rhetoric. They say I make good arguments. It's so true that I could say that, if it were up to me."

---Saint Devil, June 2015.

"Some people are confused. They ask he's really not a saint he's really more of a devil. But I give my usual excuse, and say that I invented perpetual motion- -and all saints are devils. I just don't want to be martyred. Martyr is murder. So the only saint is saint devil."

---Saint Devil, June 2015.

"The Bible is a book of luck. Whoever disagrees with this view is going to have a hard time."

--- Saint Devil

SNEAKY ENGINEER

---...Famously unpopular until his information improves---

This is Nathan Coppedge's perpetual motion archetype, originally called Eucaleh Terrapin, a kind of sublime writer and artificer of blueprints. Someone who would 'like to spill ink'. A polymath and dogmatist. An intellectual dog and romantic hero. A thin man, a 'calligraph' or calligrapher who collects many pages on his path to immortality. His ambition is to build a library to rival Alexandria. But he is a sort of devil. He wishes to do everything with originality. Life holds infinite promise, but it has certain conditions... Life is infinitely specific. In his life, the philosopher is a secret king, a relative of the Illuminati, a maker of divine symbols. His greatest project (currently) is to design many perpetual motion machines. A plan he believes he succeeds at marvelously... He is not really a fool, he is a paradoxical fool. A kind of genius. He has followed the Coppedge Curve...

"While they were floundering,
I was pondering:

No more wandering through the dark tunnels
Of grim determination!
For no; it is time to grow in a thousand -folded folds!
For which we need an infinite fuel!
(Such as perpetual motion)”

“Part of conversation is self-affirmation:
It’s definitive to be crazy,
It’s nice to be lazy...”

“About opinions: some aim to glimpse them,
Some aim to eclipse them...”
---Eucaleh Terrapin

“The ideal metaphysics is beyond criticism”
---Eucaleh Terrapin

“A different being...
A different feeling...
A different learning...
A different leaning...”
---Eucaleh Terrapin

“An image is one or two dimensional,

Because it relies on the informational"
---Eucaleh Terrapin

"They want to acquire immortality
By improving mortally---
I think that's a low blow,
As far as the cosmic scene goes..."
---Eucaleh Terrapin

"In an artificial location half truths are whole truths with good occasion"
---Eucaleh Terrapin

"Oh you know reality /
Its greed that leaves its mark /
Scars are fate and just remarks"
---Eucaleh Terrapin

"I became one of those people who said something somehow that was understandable"
---Eucaleh Terrapin

"Meanings are not vain to those that mean"
---Eucaleh Terrapin

"We learn to put 'volition' on a pedestal, but there is no real reason to put it there, except to sound intellectual" ---Eucaleh

"I was scared of teaching, it led me to better thinking"
---Eucaleh Terrapin

"Much is the stuff of literature that wishes simply to have very healthy water"
---Eucaleh Terrapin

"Sisyphus is a shadow of the desire of virtuous teenagers"
---Eucaleh Terrapin

"I thought, if I were a wight or something, I might live immortally in time"
---Eucaleh Terrapin

"In a way it isn't jealousy, its an attempt at mental energy"
---Eucaleh Terrapin

"The proof is so much what they mean and it is so much what I am"
---Eucaleh Terrapin

"So many paradises are like pieces of paper"
---Eucaleh Terrapin

"I continue in vain
In a vain of reading"
---Eucaleh Terrapin

"If you can't disagree with me, I can be insane legally"
---Eucaleh Terrapin

"Noumenology is too linguistic
to include in 'metaphysics'... "
---Eucaleh Terrapin

"If I have no authority, why am I a priority?"
---Eucaleh Terrapin

"An older song / Where things were heartsick mended wrong"---Eucaleh Terrapin

"I write the wicker---Lying like Nietzsche /
Who continues to the point?
Someone's sand-dollar watercolor ma-

chine"
---Eucaleh Terrapin

"Same groves, same bees
Things forsaken, fallen trees"
---Eucaleh Terrapin

"Not taken out to laundry /
Not pieces of matter, not aught /
Archeaology"
---Eucaleh Terrapin

"Not gambling, not rhymon meter /
Weird erosions where everythings mat-
ter"
---Eucaleh Terrapin

"Are we speaking of old men, or things
as strange /
As politics or enjoying ourselves? /
There are things that matter like /
The memory of lemonade"
---Eucaleh Terrapin

"Things like gambling /
Which are mere weather,
and blown away anyway by things that
matter"
---Eucaleh Terrapin

“Fact is easily maintained; maintenance easily has a conscience; conscience easily has a name; name easily has higher fact”

“Considering the services I receive, I could have much more prestige!”

“All original things are propositional; or if not propositional then extraordinary or ordinary; otherwise correlative;”

“The extraordinary creates the ordinal; the remnants are extraordinary too; what is not haiku may be the news”

“Haiku are formally informal; they make extraordinary facts seem normal; they abbreviate the news”

“News is informally formal; it makes propositions normal”

“Its about the nature of deliberating: no one thinks about it properly”

"So who says Non /
When nothing is an epigmemnon"
---Eucaleh Terrapin

"And feathers to the truth /
Like things were all decided in the news"
---Eucaleh Terrapin

"I'll tell you a secret though
I wasn't born an entertainer"
---Eucaleh Terrapin

"Like that to the stalwart mind of a teenager /
Is the nature of Rhebus /
Since meaningful emporiums are for intellectuals /
When not all is rice paper and spelled in chemicals"
---Eucaleh Terrapin

"Be wise: predict wisdom
(there's the rub)"
---Eucaleh Terrapin

"And tell you pinkly that reason is cribbage or garbage /

It all makes sense in the Barbilege..."
---Eucaleh Terrapin

"That's one answer: be immune to cancer"
---Eucaleh Terrapin

"That's kind of a cool building, let's
turn it into something interesting"
---Eucaleh Terrapin

"Statistical methodology is not dimensional philosophy"
---Eucaleh Terrapin

"Perpetual motion machines aren't illegal,
Contrary to conventional people"
---Eucaleh Terrapin

"Wu bei is what devils always say"
---Eucaleh Terrapin

"Selling yourself for evil is
sometimes illegal----
Never desireable,
Often medieval----
Spiritually inconceivable---
A game for pretty people"

---Eucaleh Terrapin

"Those that discover pain can sometimes discover the painful economy"
---Eucaleh Terrapin

"They think I can't have sex because
I'm embarrassed
I think that's hilarious"
---Eucaleh Terrapin

"When we're bad,
Maybe we've been had"
---Eucaleh Terrapin

"The best progress is process"
---Eucaleh Terrapin

FURTHER READING

DRAMATIS PERSONAE (PAST-LIFE STORIES)

THE LESSONS OF THE MASTER (MASTER KUO, PSEUD.)

THE STORY OF MASTER WU (MASTER KUO, PSEUD.)

THE ONE-PAGE-CLASSICS

SOULS FROM THE LIBRARY OF ALEXANDRIA

AND MANY MORE BY NATHAN COPPEDGE

BIO

Nathan Coppedge is a philosopher, artist, inventor, and poet in some capacity. He is the author of over 80 books, and has been quoted on and offline. He is a member of the International Honor Society for Philosophy, and lives in New Haven.

www.ingramcontent.com/pod-product-compliance
Lightning Source LLC
Chambersburg PA
CBHW060406290526
45791CB00002B/635

* 9 7 8 1 5 1 6 8 3 8 9 1 2 *